DIVINE COMPREHENSION

DIVINE COMPREHENSION

By Ladaro Pennix

Published by
MIDNIGHT EXPRESS BOOKS

DIVINE CONPREHENSION

Published by
MIDNIGHT EXPRESS BOOKS
POBox 69
Berryville AR 72616
(870) 210-3772
MEBooks1@yahoo.com

DIVINE COMPREHENSION

By Ladaro Pennix

Doubt

Doubt is self defeat, a defeat you should never accept.

Never give into your doubt.

It is a mind manipulator that deceives you into believing that you can't do something before you even try.

Doubt prepares you to fail while accepting the doubt means you have chosen to fail.

Be confident in all you do. Even if the outcome is undetermined go all out for you only live once.

*I live in confidence
so that doubt never declares victory over me.*

Ladaro Pennix

At Peace

*Just because the waters are calm doesn't mean you're at peace.
It only means nothing has happened yet to test your peace.*

How do you know you are strong enough to be at peace even when the unexpected happens? True knowledge of peace is attained when the tribulations of life hits you square between the eyes and you face it without missing a step. The body of peace comes from the acceptance of life's experiences and the rejection of ego defining those experiences. This is the way you mold your calm into being. Saying you're at peace doesn't count. It is living in your own calm that speaks the most volumes.

My waters remain calm even when disturbed.

Ladaro Pennix

My Deeds

My deeds mirror my internal.

You are a reflection of what you do. If you are positive, you will do positive things.

If you are negative, you will attach yourself to the chaos and misery you manifest. Our actions tell the core of us. Though our mouths may lie, our actions don't. It is through our actions do we amplify the nature of our inner selves... If people are saying you are scandalous it is because your actions are showing these traits. If they say you are a good person, it is because your work in life is pure and so you are mirroring the best part of you, your goodness. You dictate how the world sees you. No one else does.

What you give is what people will receive
whether you are good or whether you are ugly.

Ladaro Pennix

My Mistakes

I am a mountain of good and only a pebble of mistakes.

Never allow your mistakes to define the totality of who you are. So many forget all the good they have contributed to the world before tripping over their own feet and stumbling.

Never let the stumble determine the values of your life. A stumble is just that, a stumble.

Should you fall in the process, dust your knees off and get back up. There is more good to be done on your behalf.

I left my mistakes in yesterday
to progress in the good of today.

Ladaro Pennix

The Test

Test me and I will live up to my potential.

Every test is not designed to break you, but to allow your potential to flourish.

How do you know you are strong if you have never been tested? We are all at our best when the season of test arises. Every test is a defining moment that lays out the blueprint to whether or not we are worthy to know the audacity of our capacity to exceed our limits of expectation. This will tell you if you're ready to proceed in life and on to the next test.

To test me is to know me at my best.

Ladaro Pennix

My Presence

I'm not supposed to be here, but I'm here.

The world is rough and unforgiving. Sometimes, it takes us to a point of wits end where we don't need to be. Those are the times when we must push on and refuse to yield to the current of circumstances that have bombarded our piece of mind with the nonsense of a folly world gone mad. Though we are above the influence of the negative, we are only human and must realize that even though this world is rough and not on our level of maturity, we must make do, and teach the world how to be a better place.

He who is crazy enough to believe
he can change the world, usually are the ones that do.

Ladaro Pennix

Your Belief

Impose your belief on self not on others
that way you don't become a repellant to something
designed to change lives for the better.

People have for gotten how to extend the benefit of their knowledge; and so, when they offer a fabric of their insight it becomes an intrusive rant that falls upon deaf ears. Your beliefs are exactly that (your) beliefs, so to assume that everyone should adopt such belief is a naive conceit that only bullies adopt. If you desire someone to be receptive to something that's good, it is best to live the belief, so that it may set precedent and inspire them to yearn to follow in your footsteps.

Let my walk in life be the motivation
to changing lives for the better, and not my fanatic rants.

Ladaro Pennix

Know It Alls

There is a saying only fools act like they know it all, while
the real know it alls, act like they're the fools.

A man who stands in the conceit of being a "know-it-all" knows nothing but the narrow mindedness in which he stands upon. To be a know-it-all is to reject all, for you then close your mind to anything outside of the scope of which you know. That makes you the fool... The ones who actually do know-it-all are the ones who portray the role of the naiveté, allowing the class of their status to be that of a student of life as life becomes their professor. They need not the accolade of the title of being a know-it-all, because they know that that there is no such thing for learning is an infinite process that exceeds all life times.

I must learn all about nothing
in order to gain the knowledge about something.

Ladaro Pennix

Opportunities

Opportunities are blessings for the taking...seize them.

There is no opportunity that comes by coincidence. Opportunities happen because you attracted that blessing one way or another. To deny the opportunities is to deny your blessings. And when your blessings are denied, they move on to the next deserving soul who will appreciate that which you could not. Every opportunity is a blessing that you should clutch with both hands because you may not get a second chance to arrest such a moment of favorable happenings.

In the presence of opportunity,
I will not forsake what is rightfully mine.

Ladaro Pennix

Your Ego

*The ego is a fascinating phenomenon.
It could make you great or be your downfall
depending on the power you give it.*

When you allow your ego to become superior over your common sense you will find yourself in many reckless conclusions. The ego is a stubborn entity that needs its balance in order to play a significant role in your life that complements your potential. When you reject the equilibrium of ego, you cause yourself to lean too far in the direction of the extreme leaving no neutral body of thought to rationalize or create a reasonable judgment. This will create a downward spiral towards an abyss of no reprieve. But giving ego a balance allows it to enrich the ingredients of your inherent aptitude establishing the drive you need to reach endless possibilities in your quest for success. This is why the power you give ego is the power it will manifest. So be wise of the energy you give to it.

*I keep my ego in a state of balance
so that it won't get beside itself.*

Ladaro Pennix

A Wise Man

*A wise man never stops learning
for he knows that wisdom is infinite.*

There is no such thing as wisdom or knowledge or experience having a destination. All are illimitable continuums that are voided of a terminal station. It is he who dwell in that reality that knows that life's wisdoms proceed far beyond the study of text books, and that to limited yourself to one genre of learning and declare that you are superior in wisdom only shows you are inferior to the reality that what you know has yet to evolve. In essence, you know nothing at all. This is why learning never stops because every day is a new day to learn something new about what you think you know already.

*Like a child, I will look at each new day as a learning
experience
to further my progress in wisdom.*

Ladaro Pennix

Women

Upon the bosom of women lies comfort for man to rest their head upon in times when life gets too heavy to endure alone.

All women of the world possess an innate strength so extraordinary it has the ability to nurture or lift up, and inspire even the strongest of man. Without women, who are we? Empty vessels with too much testosterone doomed to self destruct. We cannot do it all by ourselves. There are times when we need the gift of a woman to bless us with her presence so that they can bring in the calm and rejuvenate our own misplace common sense and lapse of tenacity from when the world chews us up and spits us back out worn and broken...Women are truly the greatest gift to man for they complement our strength and give us the drive to be at our best.

I am never weak for I have a woman to keep me ever strong.

Ladaro Pennix

Insults

Those who insult you lack the integrity of being a builder and are usually intimidated by your success. Let them insult, and use their jealousy as a propeller to gain you an even greater momentum of success.

Jim Brown once said, "All the critics and naysayers I feed off of, I take in their criticism and hate, and digest it, then turn it into the fuel I need to motivate my determination to succeed." One should recognize insults for what they are; fuel to inspire! Do not allow the insults of the jealous and weak to intimidate or alter your greater purpose in life. Most people who insult you, do so because they are jealous of you and are frustrated at themselves as to why they are unable to reach such feats of achievement as you have. The more they hate, the more you should smile because their insults tells you that you are doing something right...succeeding in areas where they cannot.

I shall not be moved by insults,
only driven by my will to succeed.

Ladaro Pennix

Love

Submit to nothing in life but love. For love is God, respect, romance and happily ever afters all rolled up in one.

There is nothing in life more worthy to submit to than love. Love is awe inspiring. It is a gift from beyond the stars that has the capacity to knock you to your knees when you least expect it. Love is God in the sense that it is universal unmatched by any force known to mankind. Love is respect for without it love has no root. Love is romance, a nostalgic sentiment of courtship that leaves the heart suspended in a state of nirvana. Love is happily everafters that encapsulates all the beauties and wonders that love entails. Love has power and to have that power is to be in love, for love is truly the force to be reckoned with.

I will love so that it will love me back.

Ladaro Pennix

Jeckles

Read between the lines when dealing with jeckles;
their actions speak more truth than their words.

When dealing with the jeckles of the world, the easiest way to weed them out is by to watch if their actions coincide with what they say. Most jeckles say one thing and then go behind your back and do another. They are sly imps with a thick face and a black heart. They are the Judas of the world who are miserable and seek as much company as they can create for they refuse to be miserable by themselves. As deceivers and chaos mongers, they are addicted to the dramas of life's scandals and are usually the key element in the malicious gossip and slander. Be observant and read between the lines of the jeckles who come your way.

If I see the truth, I know the truth.
This truth allows me to see
through the jeckles' lies and deceit.

Ladaro Pennix

Your Phenomenal Self

Do not give your energy away to the chaos-mongers of the world who prey on your flaws for their own amusement. Protect it at all costs so that you remain consistent in your thrive towards your vision of extraordinary.

Know your phenomenal self. Do not make it a secret from yourself. When you know you are phenomenal, you will go off into the world and do phenomenal things. When you know your phenomenal self, you must then know that in order to secure your phenomenal self within the realm of your extraordinary, you must deny the chaos-mongers an opening so that they are incapable of converting your inner bliss into a corrupt misrepresentation of ill-perception of yourself and of the world. Do not give chaos-mongers a home within your mind. As an infectious disease their toxic will spread and you will find yourself an emotional wreck from the emotional rollercoaster they put you through.

I am phenomenal which makes me extraordinary. Nothing can alter that.

Ladaro Pennix

Your Struggle

You are amazing, even when you are at your worse for that is when your true tenacity shines as you overcome that which was intended for you to fail.

When struggle happens, you rise to the occasion. You show up even when you are afraid or uncertain of the outcome. You remain in the moment regardless of how defeated you might feel. Right when you are on the brink of your last will to push on you still give it all you got. Ultimately, you overcame what was meant for you to fail. How can you not know that you're amazing? Struggle is designed to create a defeatist mentality. To create the blemish of self doubt, but when you expunge the notion of being unworthy to triumph over struggle you find yourself to be champion and victor over that which attempted to manipulate you to believe that you couldn't win. That is why you are amazing!

With every struggle, I amaze myself at how amazingly tough I really am.

Ladaro Pennix

Your Storm Your Purpose

Everyone has a purpose even if they don't know it yet. That purpose is there. It is when we lose perspective of self that we lose our entitled purpose and corrupt our own awesome destiny.

What is your purpose? To know your purpose is to know your potential. We all have a purpose in life no matter how big or small that purpose exists. Our lack of acquisition is only prevalent when we deny the relevance of its significance. To deny such an important element of our lives is to ignore the importance of self for without a purpose what is there to live for? Without the embracing of our purpose, we bury our entitlement and become zombies (living dead) vessels who are just wasting their life away walking in a direction to nowhere.. .our destiny is clear when our purpose is validated. Do not corrupt your destiny by disregarding what gives your life the most substance.

My purpose is clear and with both hands I clutch and bring forth relevance.

Every storm has a beginning and an ending. Learn from it so that you will possess the know-how to conquer future storms.

Whatever you go through in life make sure you seize the opportunity to learn from it. History has a way of repeating itself, and the more you learn from past struggles the easier it is to triumph over present and future struggles. Storms will be storms. They are meant to complicate things in your life. With the know-how to face them no matter how challenging the weather might be, you will get through it effortlessly. For Just as a storm begins, you know it will quickly ends.

Through any weather, I will survive.

Waves of Life

*The waves of life have the ability to knock you to your knees.
That is why we must learn to swim to avoid drowning when
our footing is swept from beneath us.*

The interesting thing about life is that you never truly see it coming. What I mean is life is there, but it is only transparent to a point to a certain degree. The rest of it is a hazy mist and fog that creeps upon you and surprises you when you least expect it. These are the harsh waves that have the ability to uproot your very foundation and challenge the core of your overall stability. In those moments, you must learn to swim on your own while at the same time avoid the currents that pull you deeper into the oceans waves that submerge you deeper beneath the salty waters floor. When you learn to swim, even when you are knocked off your feet, there's no worry because you know that your arms are strong enough to overcome the waves of life. So swim on and let nothing stop you!

*I know how to swim.
That's why you will never see me drown!*

Ladaro Pennix

Obstacle

Every great obstacle has challenged me to never give up on life. Call me stubborn, but no foe will ever claim such victory of causing me to quit just because they have complicated my existence.

I come from a long line of hard-knocks who refused to ever accept a defeatist mentality.

My personality has not always been a favorable one and so my foe's have always been many. There have been times when my foe's joined allegiance with each other to take me out of the picture through some grand scheme of strategy. Assuming to make history in my defeat, they miscalculated one thing. I am not moved by any of the antics my foes may conjure up, and so the end result is here I stand stronger than ever in my resolve to remain firm and ever rebellious towards any foe who dares to test my will and tenacious spirit.

My mind is like a rock.
My heart is steel.
There is no foe that can break me.

Ladaro Pennix

Mothers

All mothers are super-heroes. They may not be able to leap from tall buildings and fly, but the sacrifice they make for their kids is superhero awesome.

Mothers of the world are marvelous sensations who deserve all the accolades that a superhero has acquired. Indeed, all mothers are superheroes themselves for to raise a child into an adult takes tremendous superhuman abilities that only a mother could possess. For them to not be acknowledged for their hard work and tough skin would be a disservice to mankind as a whole. Mothers of the world do all the things those fathers won't or can't do. They separate their ego so that it doesn't get in the way of raising their child/children because of it, they are able to love us unconditionally without stipulations or limitations. Mothers are the best. Don't you agree?

I exalt all mothers with praise for you are truly the superheroes of the world.

Ladaro Pennix

Balance

The other side of sanity is insanity.
Where does the line border before you find yourself
too far off into the deep-end?

We are always on the verge of insanity. The only thing that keeps us sane is the balance on the tightrope which borders the dualistic paradigms of each polar extreme. If we lean too far on either side, we alter the balance and cause the positive to turn into a negative, in such case, the extremes of the polarities no longer balance in the mixture and you find yourself in the pool of two-kinds of insanity, "The one you are aware of, and the one you're not." This is why the balance is imperative so that one never falls too much into either dualistic polar extremes and lose themselves in the process.

My balance is my harmony. My harmony is my balance.

Ladaro Pennix

Critics

*Not all critics are parasites.
Some are actually teachers
helping you to better your potential.*

Although many critics only criticize you to tear you down, not all possess that insidious ritual of feeding off others misery as a means of some self-satisfying exaltation of downing the next to make themselves feel like something of importance. There are actually critics out there who want to see you make it. They want to see you at your best. So they give you an honest opinion so that you may see your shortcomings and step your game up so that your flaw transforms into a strength that leads you towards greater feats of achievement. Learn to differentiate the two so that you can be receptive to one and disregard the other.

This will challenge your potential and show you how to be at your best.

*I am not afraid of criticism
for it teaches me how to improve in all that I do.*

Ladaro Pennix

Words

Words can be as deadly as a gun.
It is the man behind the words as is the man behind the gun
that makes them so dangerous.

Words are as dangerous as the people behind the words. Anyone can throw daggers, but there are people who actually shoot bullets with words wounding the core of you and sometimes killing your very spirit. Those kinds of people are dangerous for they study everything for all the wrong reasons just so they can articulate themselves in a way that assassinates the essence of who you are. These people you must not give an ear too. Let them talk, and while they're talking, you find comfort in being amazing just the way you are. It is when you give them significance that you become effected by the bullets of their words.

My peace is still when others' words no longer define me.

Ladaro Pennix

Respect

Respect goes a mighty long way. Try it sometime.

We live in a rude society where "I" and "me" are the only two things that matter to the individual. Courtesy has become obsolete, and in its place is the "give me" mentality. You give me respect. You give me this and that and "I" will take it because "I" deserve it! The only thing "I" deserve is a good kick in the rear-end for being so selfish and spoiled. It doesn't hurt to be courteous. It doesn't cost to show respect to others. Respect has become a lost form. Too many people correlate respect to being weak or soft. Respect has nothing to do with weakness but everything to do with being a human being and possessing the core values of being considerate. In that, understand you will receive a genuine reciprocation of the same esteem you mirror to the world.

I respect "me" so I will respect the "we" of society.

Ladaro Pennix

My Spirits

When my spirits are sap of motivation and life becomes too unbearable, I reflect on all that I have overcome and smile at how much of a tough ass I really am.

Make no mistake, you are here breathing and living for a reason. Think about all that you have been through; every road block, every painful experience, every life altering moment that wounded you in ways you never thought possible. Did you not survive? Did you not come out on the other end stronger than you came in? You are unbreakable because you refuse to be a victim of circumstance. This shows the audacity of your toughness and an innate strength that will take you far. When you're down, just simply recall all the moments that you were worst off and how you made it through. If that doesn't lift your spirits, I don't know what will.

If you keep in mind what you endured yesterday, you will know you have what it takes to overcome the problems of today.

Ladaro Pennix

Listening

I listen to learn.
That's why I adopted the art of talking less.

When you're not talking, you're listening. When you listen, you learn that by not talking you are able to hear what people say and gain a full comprehension of what's being expressed to you. A lot of people when they're engaged in discourse, they are too caught up in their own desire to express their opinions(s) that they ignore the beneficial information shared with them that could possibly teach them something. An earlier scholar once said, "A close mouth doesn't get fed." Though that is true, in some cases, when it comes to listening that does not apply because a close mouth feeds the mind especially when you are open to listen to what's being said to you. So talk less, and listen more. You might learn something

Today my mouth is closed
and my ears are receptive to listening.

My Intelligence

*Though I am intelligent, I play dumb a lot
in order to find out a lot.*

Most people believe me to be so smart that I'm stupid. This is because so much is done behind the scenes and because I do not speak about it they believe the wool is pulled over my eyes. There is a time and a place for everything. Sometimes you have to pass up opportunities to address your adversaries in order to obtain better opportunities worth the taking. As I play dumb, much is revealed for my foe(s) become cocky in their schemes and begin showing their hands and allowing their tongues to run away from them. Believing I'm too dumb to pick up their subtle darts that they throw in my direction, I catch them, put them in my pocket, and save them for ammunition for when it's my time to shine.

*If a man plays dumb, is he actually dumb or is the real
dummies the ones who actually believe he is?*

Ladaro Pennix

A Warrior

Don't be a warrior in a silent army of fools.

The worse mistake a warrior can make is caring about the opinions of fools. You can not be a warrior amongst a silent army of fools. It will only make you look like a fool yourself. A true warrior needs not prove a thing to fools. Any fool can talk hard, and act hard, but a warrior is one who knows who he is without emphasis on effort. Amid a silent army of fools, a warrior must humble himself so that he doesn't find himself caught up in the hype of fools and ultimately a victim of his own stupidity.

I shall let the fools be fools while I play my part in closing the door to being a fool myself.

Ladaro Pennix

About the Author

Ladaro J. Pennix, II, a Southern California native raised in Long Beach California. He studies psychology and business. A humanitarian at heart, his basic instinct is helping people through conscious awareness that promotes self-reform.

Pennix has written several books such as *Character and Ethics*, *Love Torch*, *Sugar for My Granny Editions*, and soon to come, the thriller novel *The Sway*.

He currently resides in northern California.

Ladaro Pennix

www.ingramcontent.com/pod-product-compliance
Lightning Source LLC
Chambersburg PA
CBHW071851020426

42331CB00007B/1960